C0-BXA-266

Britta,
Wishing you all the best.
I'm so thankful our paths
crossed.
Tracye

What 'Cha Think About This

Recipes Using Tracye's Chicken Salad Dressing
Delicious Recipes That Are Not So Chicken

Tracye Carter

AuthorHouse™
1663 Liberty Drive
Bloomington, IN 47403
www.authorhouse.com
Phone: 1 (800) 839-8640

© 2016 Tracye Carter. All rights reserved.

No part of this book may be reproduced, stored in a retrieval system,
or transmitted by any means without the written permission of the author.

Published by AuthorHouse 01/27/2016

ISBN: 978-1-5049-6784-6 (sc)
ISBN: 978-1-5049-6783-9 (hc)
ISBN: 978-1-5049-6785-3 (e)

Library of Congress Control Number: 2015920793

Print information available on the last page.

Any people depicted in stock imagery provided by Thinkstock are models,
and such images are being used for illustrative purposes only.
Certain stock imagery © Thinkstock.

This book is printed on acid-free paper.

Because of the dynamic nature of the Internet, any web addresses or links contained in this book may have changed
since publication and may no longer be valid. The views expressed in this work are solely those of the author and do not
necessarily reflect the views of the publisher, and the publisher hereby disclaims any responsibility for them.

author**HOUSE**

DEDICATION

This book is dedicated to Mommy, Norma Carter. Mommy instilled in me to march to the beat of God's drum and in doing so, I can do anything! Mommy this one's for you!

With Love,

Miss Molly

ACKNOWLEDGEMENTS

Thanks to my brother, Roy for sacrificing and helping me whenever, wherever and whatever; you're the best!

Ms. Julia, thanks for your support and humor. Thanks for pushing my dressing into the hands of so many people.

Janay Thomas, thank you for working with so much passion and vigor.

For their energy, enthusiasm, love, patience, support and humor, I thank my family and friends.

Table of Contents

INTRODUCTION

THIS BOOK is filled with recipes I have developed using my dressing. Yes, I originally developed this dressing exclusively to prepare chicken salad, only to discover the dressing can be used on vegetables, seafood, pork, beef and more. The possibilities are endless when using my dressing. It can be used to make cold dips and dishes as well as hot side dishes and the main course. It's amazing! My dressing is like a chameleon because an entire meal can be prepared using it, from the salad to the entrée. The dressing adapts a different taste! The dressing is so flavorful that it minimizes buying other herbs and spices because everything you'll need is already in the dressing! Eating healthy doesn't mean food should be bland. Nor does eating healthy mean spending hours in the kitchen.

In *What 'Cha Think About This,* I share recipes using my dressing that will create ease to your busy schedules. Most of the recipes are prepared in 20 minutes or less. A generous amount of pictures and easy to follow instructions are also included to make it super easy for you to get out of the kitchen in record time.

I hope you find a recipe that you absolutely enjoy, so much that you share it with your family and friends. I pray you have good eating experiences and great conversations along the way. May the blessing of connecting the good things of the past to the gift of the present along with the possibilities of what is to come be yours.

THE BEGINNING...

In 1988 I moved to Georgia because it had the perfect atmosphere to start a business. It didn't take me long to decide on a domestic based venture. In 1992 I started a cleaning company. One of my clients was having guests over for a holiday open house and she asked me if I knew someone who could help warm hors oeuvres, and keep the table looking great for her Guests. Of course I took the job! The news traveled fast of the great job I did, so more and more people starting calling for us to work for them, helping their entertainment at home experience run smoothly. Why not feel like a guest at your own party? The client list grew rapidly throughout the Atlanta metropolitan area. 1994 is a notable year because Simply Elegance Catering was born.

My catering style effortlessly developed into a more healthy fare with a presentation of *simple elegance*. In 2006 a client ordered chicken salad on croissants for a small luncheon at her law office. Well, I must confess, growing up in Racine, Wisconsin, we were not a "chicken salad" town. I'd say, "I'm a tuna girl," I grew up eating tuna fish sandwiches. The closest we'd come to chicken salad was after Thanksgiving. Mommy would utilize the extra turkey and make turkey salad. The turkey salad sandwiches were so good but it wasn't chicken. Anyway, I delivered the chicken salad on croissants and they loved it.

For every gathering I was invited to they'd tell me to bring chicken salad. People raved about my chicken salad for years. I really thought people were just being nice in giving compliments about the chicken salad. When friends would ask for my recipe, I wouldn't give it to them because as a caterer, I didn't want my recipe floating all over town. There would be no need for them to order it from me, right?

Finally, I began to believe that my friends and clients were really serious and not just being polite. I began to believe in my God-given creation. I began visiting notable eateries and food markets known for their chicken salad. I realized that my chicken salad was "the bomb…BOOM!"

In January 2013 a friend insisted I explore the avenues of putting my chicken salad in grocery stores. As I pondered the thought, God gave me the idea to put the chicken salad dressing on the market and then people can make their own at their leisure. After all, chicken is tasteless-the dressing dresses the chicken! The rest is history! Tracye's Culinary Creations Chicken Salad Dressing hit the scene. The dressing followed suit with my healthy catering style. My dressing can be utilized by most because it contains **NO CARBS, NO SUGAR, NO TRANSFATS, NO ARTIFICIAL PRESERVATIVES, GLUTEN FREE AND DAIRY FREE.** It contains egg. However, eggs are not dairy. I point this out because markets generally position eggs and milk together, confusing some consumers.

June 22, 2013, Tracye's Chicken Salad Dressing was put on the first store shelf-**Maliki's Piggly Wiggly** in Racine, WI. August 23, 2013 my dressing went on the shelf of **Wayfield Foods** a local grocery store chain throughout Atlanta. On November 30, 2013 Tracye's Chicken Salad Dressing graced the shelves of **Whole Foods Markets** and **Harry's Farmers Market**, and on December 3, 2013 we were put on the shelves of **Sendiks Food Market**.

It's been an incredible journey and I hope you hop on board and join me by trying the recipes in my cookbook; the first of many to come.

For additional information about my dressing and where it may be purchased please visit **www.tracyEcarter.com**.

THE CHICKEN SALAD

For years clients and friends alike have repeatedly asked me to make chicken salad or "how do you get your chicken so tender," Well, the recipe below will help you achieve a duplication of my chicken salad!

TRACYE'S ULTIMATE CHICKEN SALAD

6-8 Servings

Poached chicken

4 cups chicken breasts
1 onion
2 carrots peeled
2 celery stalks

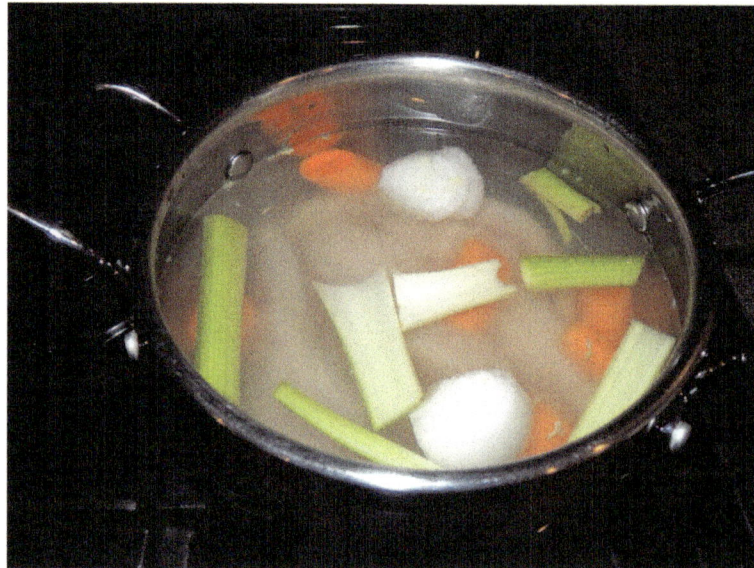

Pot of poaching Chicken

Poach the chicken. Place the chicken breasts in a large pot and cover the breast with water, Place chunks of celery, onion and carrots in the pot as well and bring water to a boil. Turn down to low/medium and simmer for 1 hour. Turn heat off, place a lid on the pot and let it stand for at least 30 minute.

Remove chicken from the water, discarding the onion, celery and carrots.

Place the chicken in a bowl and break the chicken up using your hands. The chicken should be tender enough to fall apart.

Add chopped onions, celery, dried cranberries and Granny Smith apples to the bowl of chicken.

½ cup finely chopped onions
¼ cup finely chopped celery,
1 cup dried cranberries
1 Granny Smith apple finely chopped
1 jar Tracye's Chicken Salad Dressing*

Add ½ jar Tracye's Chicken Salad Dressing and stir. If needed add more dressing until it is to your desired wetness and stir.

Vegetarian option- use a mock breadless chicken substitute, break it down to tiny pieces, add the fruits, vegetables and chicken salad dressing, it's delicious.

Tee Notes – *When chopping I use a food processor and chop until the fruit or vegetable is almost "mushy" You obtain the flavor without the crunch.*

A chicken salad bar would be a great addition to any gathering; have martini glasses available, allow guests to add the fruits and/or vegetables of their choice.

Notes

TEE'S TEASERS

ALL MIXED UP

EASY AVOCADO DIP

TRACYE'S DEVILISH EGGS

SPINACH TARTLETS

TWISTED COLLARD GREEN DIP

All Mixed Up serves as a party dip and a salad dressing. It's extremely simple and easy to make and you actually can make as much or as little as you want; simply by mixing equal parts of Tracye's Chicken Salad Dressing and plain non-fat yogurt. Yes, it's just that simple. Put equal parts in a bowl; stir it up and pour it on your green salad. For a slight hint of "kick" I add red pepper flakes. The bacon kicks it to another level!

ALL MIXED UP

Serves 8 to 10

½ cup Tracye's Chicken Salad Dressing
½ cup low fat plain yogurt
¼ teaspoon red pepper flakes (optional)
½ tablespoon bacon bits (optional)

In a mixing bowl, combine Tracye's Chicken Salad Dressing and the low fat yogurt. Mix well

Add the red pepper flakes and bacon bits to taste. Cover and chill

Notes

Notes

Add this to your recipe collection. It is super easy to prepare and no cooking is required!

EASY AVOCADO DIP

Makes 2 cup

2 Ripe Avocado (peeled and pitted – save the pit)
1/2 cup Tracye's Chicken Salad Dressing
1/2 cup non-fat plain yogurt
1 cup Chunky Salsa
½ teaspoon ground cumin
Fresh Cilantro to taste (optional)

In a medium bowl, mash the avocados with a potato masher. Mix in Tracye's Chicken Salad Dressing, yogurt, salsa and cumin. Chill at least 30 minutes before serving.

Serve with tortilla chips toasted bread or fresh veggies.

Tee Notes – *To prevent browning, place the avocado pit into the container. Store the avocado dip and avocado pit in an air tight container until you are ready to serve, Remove avocado pit prior to serving.*

Notes

Notes

One evening while the TCC team was hard at work I went in the kitchen and made these delicious eggs. I know the recipe seems long but in actuality within this recipe are "how to" instructions on how to cook a hard boil egg and more. These devilish eggs are good!

TRACYE'S DEVILISH EGGS

Makes 24 pieces

1 dozen eggs
1/2 cup Tracye's Chicken Salad Dressing
2 tablespoons sweet pickle relish
1/4 teaspoon ground black pepper
4 strips of low sodium bacon
Fresh chives
Paprika
Chili powder for an extra kick (optional)

Preheat oven 400 degrees.

Arrange the bacon on a foil lined baking sheet (this makes clean-up easier). Lay bacon on the baking sheet in a Single layer – do not overlap. Place the baking sheet of bacon in the oven and bake until the bacon is deep golden-brown and crisp, approximately 15-20 minutes. Cooking time will depend on the thickness of the bacon. **No need to turn bacon

When the bacon is done, remove the bacon from the oven and use tongs to transfer to a paper-lined plate to drain and finish crisping.

Place the eggs in a large saucepan and pour in enough cold water to cover by 1 inch.

Bring to a boil over high heat. Remove from the heat, cover, and set aside for 15 minutes. While eggs are cooking, keep an eye on the bacon.

Transfer eggs to a colander; place under cool running water to stop the cooking. Cool completely and peel.

Cut the eggs in half lengthwise and remove the yolks. Keep the halves of the whites intact.

Place the yolks in a medium sized bowl and mash the yolks. Add remaining ingredients and mix until smooth.

Mound a heaping spoonful of the yolk mixture into the cavity of the whites. Garnish with crumbled bacon, paprika and fresh chives

Tee Notes – *Bacon may be replaced by bacon bits. Try these variations to make an assortment of Tracye's Devilish Eggs:*

Crumble blue cheese to the egg yoke mixture.

Combine the yolk mixture with red curry paste and mango chutney for a bright and tangy mixture

Top Tracye's Devilish Eggs with pesto

Notes

This recipe is one you'd want to go to when you are entertaining guest. I made these for an event I catered. They're mess free, no fork needed, just grab and pop the tartlets in your mouth…You will not just eat one!

SPINACH TARTLETS

Serves 36

2 cups cream cheese
½ cup Tracye's Chicken Salad Dressing
1 ¼ cups frozen chopped spinach
1 cup Parmesan cheese, grated
3 garlic cloves, minced
1 tablespoons lemon juice
36 tartlets filo shells

Preheat oven to 375 degrees F. Drain the spinach in a colander and squeeze dry

In a medium bowl, using an electric mixer, thoroughly mix together all 6 ingredients.

Fill tartlets with the spinach filling and place on a baking sheet. Bake for 15 minutes or until filling top is lightly brown.

Notes

Notes

Collard greens with a twist. I usually only eat collards when I'm preparing dinner. Since collard greens are rich in iron, protein, fiber and vitamins, I wanted to explore how well they would taste as a dip… TEE-LICIOUS! How cool is that? Party food that's good for you…What 'Cha Think About That!!!

TWISTED COLLARD GREEN DIP

24 Servings

2 cups cream cheese
½ cup Tracye's Chicken Salad Dressing
14 oz can artichoke hearts, drained and chopped
1 ¼ cups frozen chopped collard greens, thawed & drained
1 cup Parmesan cheese, grated
3 garlic cloves, minced
2 tablespoons lemon juice

Preheat oven to 375 degrees F. Drain the greens and squeeze dry

In a medium bowl, mix together the first 5 ingredients; Season with garlic and lemon juice.

Spread evenly into a 9"x 9" baking dish. Cover and bake for 20 minutes. Remove the cover, and bake uncovered for 5 more minutes, or until the surface is lightly brown.

Serve hot with tortilla chips

Notes

Notes

SALADS

TEE-LICIOUS SALMON SALAD

TRACYE'S REAL DEAL TUNA

TUNA IMPOSTER (VEGETARIAN)

AHI MAC SALAD

BACON AND EGG SALAD

TATER SALAD

PASTA AND FRIENDS

If you're not one to crank up the oven, canned salmon will work okay, however to get the Tee-Liciousness of this salad, fresh salmon is definitely the way to go.

TEE-LICIOUS SALMON SALAD

Serves 4

2 cups fresh salmon flaked
1/3 cup green onion chopped
1/3 cup celery diced
1/3 cup Tracye's Chicken Salad dressing
Fresh ground pepper, to taste
Cucumbers, cherry tomatoes and spring mix

Directions

Preheat oven 425°

Line roasting pan with foil, place salmon fillet(s) in pan and bake uncovered for 6 minutes or until you can flake it with a fork. Remove the salmon fillet from the pan and flake it. Allow it to cool completely.

In a medium bowl, add chopped green onion, diced celery and Tracye's Chicken Salad Dressing.

Add the cooled salmon with the other ingredients; add pepper to tasted, stir to combine all the ingredients. Chill and serve.

Notes

_____

_____

_____

_____

_____

_____

_____

_____

_____

_____

_____

Notes

Growing up we ate tons of tuna fish sandwiches. It was an easy and tasty. Well this recipe is in a league of its own. It is the TRUTH! Using a fresh tuna steak instead of the beloved can will make you vow to never use can tuna ever again.

TRACYE'S REAL DEAL TUNA

4 Servings

1 fresh tuna steak
4 tablespoons sweet pickle relish
½ teaspoon curry powder
1 tablespoon dried parsley
1 teaspoon dried dill weed
1 pinch garlic powder
1/3 cup chopped onion
¼ teaspoon dried minced onion flakes
1 tablespoon Parmesan cheese
6 tablespoons Tracye's Chicken Salad Dressing

Preheat the oven to 450 degrees F. Place tuna steak on a greased baking sheet.

Bake 4 to 6 minutes per ½ inch thickness or until the fish begins to flake when tested with a fork. Remove from oven and cool completely.

Place cooled tuna steak in a medium bowl; using a fork, flake the fish. Add the remaining 9 ingredients and mix well. Increase or decrease the dressing to your desired wetness. Chill

Tee Notes – *This goes great alone, with crackers, as a sandwich or atop lettuce!*

Notes

Notes

I developed this recipe for my vegetarian clients. It's simple, easy and Tee-licious! Non vegetarians loved it also. If you have the time use dried chickpeas.

TUNA IMPOSTER *is my vegetarian version of tuna salad.*

Serves 4

1 (19oz) can garbanzo beans (chickpeas, drained and mashed)
2 tablespoons Tracye's Chicken Salad Dressing
1 tablespoon sweet pickle relish
2 green onions, chopped
½ teaspoon curry powder
Pepper to taste

In a medium bowl, put the drained garbanzo beans and mash them with a potato masher or fork. Add remaining ingredients Tracye's Chicken Salad Dressing, relish, chopped green onions, curry and pepper, mix well.

Chill and serve.

Great with crackers or on a sandwich atop bean sprouts.

Tee Notes – *If you're using dried chickpeas, cover beans with water and discard any beans that float. Cover 2 to 3 inches with water, bring to a boil; lower heat and simmer, covered until soften, about 1 ½ hours.*

Notes

This is quick, easy and to the point. It is a definite "go to" when preparing for a large crowd. I added curry because it gives it such a pleasant unique taste. You'll have to make more before you know it!

AHI MAC SALAD

Serves 8

1-8 ounce box elbow macaroni

3 eggs

½ package frozen green peas

2 –6 ounce ahi tuna steaks

1 medium onion

1 celery stalk

1/2 cup Tracye's Chicken Salad Dressing

1 teaspoon curry powder

¼ teaspoon salt

1/8 teaspoon black pepper

Prepare elbow macaroniaccording to package and rinse under cold water

Preheat the oven to 450 degrees F. Place tuna steak on a greased baking sheet.

Bake 4 to 6 minutes per ½ inch thickness or until the fish begins to flake when tested with a fork.

Remove from oven and cool

Place eggs in a saucepan and cover with cold water. Over medium heat, bring water to a full boil. Lower heat and simmer for 10-15 minutes. Immediately plunge eggs into cold water

Put frozen peas into a colander and rinse with hot water, drain well. In a large bowl place the macaroni, peas, onions and celery. Peel eggs and dice them into the bowl. Put the tuna in the bowl and flake apart.

Stir Tracye's Chicken Salad Dressing into the mixture a little at a time, until your desired wetness. Sprinkle the curry powder, salt and pepper to taste and mix one last time. Cover and refrigerate for at least one hour or overnight.

Notes

Who said bacon and eggs were only for breakfast? I absolutely love this salad. Served nestled in a buttery croissant…heavenly!

BACON AND EGG SALAD

Serves 4-6

6 eggs
¼ cup Tracye's Chicken Salad Dressing
½ teaspoon prepared yellow mustard
¼ cup chopped green onion
¼ teaspoon paprika
2 Tablespoons sweet relish
2 strips low sodium bacon (garnish)
Salt and pepper to taste

Place eggs in a saucepan and cover with cold water. Bring water to a boil and immediately remove from heat. Cover and let eggs stand in hot water for 10 to 12 minutes. Remove from hot water, cool and peel. For faster cooling, place the eggs in an ice bath before peeling.

In a medium bowl, stir together Tracye's Chicken Salad Dressing, yellow mustard and green onions. Chop the eggs in big chunks and mix gently with the dressing; season with salt and pepper. Garnish with bacon. Serve on your favorite wheat bread or cracker.

Be the talk of the social gathering when you show up with this awesome potato salad. It can be served warm or cold. I love it warm, it's finger licking good!

TATER SALAD

Serve 8

8 medium potatoes, cooked and diced

1 ½ cups Tracye's Chicken Salad Dressing

2 tablespoons cider vinegar

1 tablespoon yellow mustard

½ cup sweet pickle relish

1 teaspoon garlic powder

½ teaspoon pepper

2 celery ribs, sliced

1 cup onion, minced

5 hard-boiled eggs

Paprika

Salt and pepper to taste

Peel the potatoes, place peeled potatoes in a large pot and add enough water to cover them, (about an inch over).

Bring to a boil over high heat. Reduce heat to medium and cook until tender, about 15 to 20 minutes. A fork should easily be able to go into them. Pour the water off and allow them to cool to room temperature.

Place eggs in a saucepan and cover with cold water. Bring water to a boil and immediately remove from heat. Cover and let eggs stand in hot water for 10 to 12 minutes. Remove from hot water, cool and peel. For faster cooling, place the eggs in an ice bath before peeling.

Meanwhile, in a medium bowl, whisk together my chicken salad dressing, cider vinegar, mustard, garlic powder, pepper celery and onions. Set aside.

Dice the potatoes into cubes and place in a medium bowl. Add the dressing mixture to the potatoes, coating the potatoes. Add eggs and relish, gently mix them in with the potatoes. Sprinkle a little paprika on top for garnish. Serve immediately or chill thoroughly, at least 2 hours.

Tee Notes – I know you're dirtying up another bowl and you wonder why not just put the potatoes in the same bowl as the dressing. Here's why – If you like your salad a little dryer, you will be able to control that aspect. You can always add more dressing.

Notes

Notes

I prepared this for a friend's book signing and the guests love it. It's so pretty and colorful. With red,, orange and yellow peppers and the bright greenness of the fresh spinach; not only does it look great, it tastes amazing.

PASTA AND FRIENDS

Serves 8

1 (8oz) package uncooked pasta shells
3 cups raw spinach
½ red bell pepper, chopped
½ orange bell pepper, chopped
½ yellow bell pepper, chopped
1 cup onion finely chopped
1/3 cup black olives
1 cup cherry tomatoes (leave them whole or cut them in half)
1 jar Tracye's Chicken Salad Dressing

Cook pasta according to directions on the package.

Pour pasta in a colander, rinse with cold water, drain and place in large bowl.

Add next 7 ingredients to the pasta and add dressing starting with ½ jar, toss and continue adding more dressing as needed until you reach your desired wetness.

Chill and serve

Tee Notes – *To make this salad a main dish add a protein, for example, 3 cups chicken breast cubed or cooked shrimp*

Notes

Notes

THE MAIN EVENT

TEE'S CHICKEN AND PASTA

SIMPLE TILAPIA PARMESAN

GRILLED HALIBUT

SEARED TUNA

GRILLED CORNISH HEN

MARVELOUS MEATLOAF

CHOPS N' APPLE SAUCE

BAKED CHICKEN PARMESAN

One chilly fall evening I wanted something quick and easy to have for dinner. Being from Wisconsin, I prefer hot meals when it's cooler outside. My curiosity had much to do with my decision to see what would happen if I heated my dressing. Not really sure how I would use it, I put the chicken tenders in the skillet, put the dressing on top, boiled some pasta and my first dish was born. I think you'll love it!

TEE'S CHICKEN AND PASTA

Serves 4

4 chicken tenders
2 teaspoons olive oil
Garlic powder
Ground black pepper
8 oz bow tie pasta
½ cup Tracye's Chicken Salad Dressing

Cook the pasta according to package

Season chicken tenders on both sides with garlic and pepper to taste.

Heat olive oil in a skillet over medium heat. Place chicken in the skillet and reduce to medium heat, cook 4 minutes on each side.

Spoon Chicken Salad Dressing over chicken; spread evenly over each piece.

Cover and simmer on low heat for 10 minutes.

Heat olive oil

Place seasoned chicken in the skillet

Spread dressing over the chicken

Cover and simmer

Serving suggestion add a salad and crusty bread, you're good to go!

The simplicity of this recipe makes it even more appealing. Serve it alongside of seasoned rice and asparagus. You're ready to enjoy your meal in less than 20 minutes!

SIMPLE TILAPIA PARMESAN

Serves 4

4 Tilapia filet
½ jar Tracye's Chicken Salad Dressing
¼ cup Parmesan cheese
Black pepper

Preheat oven broiler. Spray a broiler pan with non -stick spray or line pan with aluminum foil.

In a small bowl, mix together the Parmesan cheese and Tracye's Chicken salad dressing. Mix well and set aside.

Arrange fillets in a single layer on the prepared pan.

Broil a few inches away from the heat 2 to 3 minutes. Turn the fillets over and broil for 1 to 2 minutes.

Remove the fillets from the oven and cover them with the dressing mixture on the top side.

Broil additional minutes until the topping is browned and fish flakes easily with a fork, approximately 1 ½ to 2 minutes. *Be careful not to overcook the fish.*

Notes

_____

_____

_____

_____

_____

_____

_____

_____

_____

_____

Notes

December 2014 is when I realized that the dressing can be used on just about EVERYTHING! I went to Whole Foods to perform demonstrations and allowed customers to sample salmon prepared with my chicken salad dressing. The flavor was amazing. Lemon juice is used as the preservative in my dressing. It allows the dressing to bring great flavor to any fish filet. Don't be afraid to experiment, you can't go wrong. The recipe below is with Halibut.

6 MINUTE HALIBUT

Serves 4

4 Halibut Filets
1 Jar of Tracye's Chicken Salad Dressing
Parsley for garnish

Place salad dressing on the bottom of a large skillet, use just enough dressing to place under each filet.

Place Halibut filet in the skillet, making sure each filet has dressing underneath.

Cook the fish on medium high for 2 minutes then reduce heat to medium.

The dressing will turn into oil as it heats.

Cook fish approximately 4 minutes, until golden brown, then turn fish filet and cook an additional 2 minutes. Do not overcook.

Notes

This is an elegant yet simple way to cook tuna that any restaurant would be jealous of!

SEARED TUNA

2 Servings

2 (5 ounce) tuna steaks
½ teaspoon kosher salt
¼ teaspoon cayenne pepper
½ tablespoon butter
2 tablespoons Tracye's Chicken Salad Dressing
1 teaspoon whole peppercorns

Season the tuna steaks with salt and cayenne pepper

Melt the butter with Tracye's Chicken Salad Dressing in a skillet over medium-high heat.

Cook peppercorns in the mixture until they are softened and pop, about 5 minutes. **Gently** place the seasoned tuna in the skillet and cook to desired doneness.

1 ½ minutes each side for rare

Notes

Notes

I cook weekly for senior citizens and decided to give them something a little different than the roasted Cornish hen that they were accustomed to. The flavor is amazing and the dressing sticks to the hen.

GRILLED CORNISH HEN

4 Servings

2 Cornish hens, about 1 pound each
2 medium cloves garlic, minced
½ teaspoon ground black pepper
1 jar Tracye's Chicken Salad Dressing

Cut Cornish hens in half, **Wash** hens thoroughly, pat the hens dry with paper towels, breast side down on a large cutting board.

Season all sides of the hen with garlic powder and ground black pepper. Then brush hens inside cavity with Tracye's Chicken Salad Dressing. Set aside for 15-30 minutes; the hens will cook better if they are at room temperature.

While the hens are coming to room temperature, get your grill hot. Make sure the grates are clean. Just before you put the birds on the grill, spray with non-stick oil.

Place hens on the grill, skin side up. Cover and cook for about 10 minutes. Brush Tracye's Chicken Salad Dressing on the skin side. Turn hens over, skin side down and grill until golden brown and the center of breasts registers 145 to 150° on an instant read thermometer, about 15 minutes.

Remove from grill, let stand for 5 minutes, and serve.

Notes

Notes

Every time I make this meatloaf it disappears. One day on my way home from work I decided I'd eat my leftover meatloaf instead of cooking something else. Needless to say, my sister greeted me with a plate of the meatloaf, chewing and smiling at the same time. When you make this, make sure you stash some away for yourself.

MARVELOUS MEATLOAF

8 servings

1 ½ pounds ground chuck

1 egg

1 onion, chopped

½ cup Tracye's Chicken Salad Dressing

¼ cup milk

1 cup dried bread crumbs

Salt and pepper to taste

2 tablespoons brown sugar

2 tablespoons prepared mustard

1/3 cup ketchup

Preheat oven to 350 degrees

In a large bowl, combine the beef, egg onion, Tracye's Chicken Salad Dressing, milk and bread crumbs.

Season with salt and pepper to taste

Place in a lightly greased 5 x 9 loaf pan, **OR** form meat mixture into a loaf and place in a lightly greased 9x13 inch baking dish.

Bake for 1 hour

In a separate small bowl, combine the brown sugar, mustard and ketchup; mix well and pour over the meatloaf the final 15 minutes of baking.

Notes

Notes

_____

_____

_____

_____

_____

_____

_____

_____

_____

One for all pie is what I call it. This pie is perfect for the meat and potatoes kind of gal or guy!

MEAT - POTATO PIE

Serves 6-8

1 medium potato, peeled and cubed

2 Tablespoons Tracye's Chicken Salad
   Dressing

½ pound ground chuck

½ ground pork

1/3clove garlic, chopped

½ cup onion, chopped

¼ cup water

½ teaspoon mustard powder

½ teaspoon dried thyme

¼ teaspoon ground cloves

1 teaspoon salt

¼ teaspoon ground black pepper

¼ teaspoon dried sage

1 (15 oz) package refrigerated pie
   crusts

Preheat the oven to 425 degrees. Place the potato in a saucepan with enough water to cover. Bring to a boil and cook until tender, about 6 minutes. Drain, add 2 tablespoons of Tracye's Chicken Salad Dressing, mash and set aside.

Meanwhile, crumble the ground beef and pork into a large saucepan, and add the garlic, onion and water. Season with mustard powder, thyme, cloves and salt; cook over medium heat, stirring to crumble the meat and mix the spices. Cook until the meat is evenly browned. Remove from the heat and mix in the mashed potatoes.

Place one of the pie crusts into a 9 inch pie pan. Fill with the meat mixture, then top with the other pie crust. Crimp around the edges using a fork to seal top and bottom crusts together. Trim excess dough and prick the top crust a few times with a knife to vent.

Bake until the crust is golden brown, about 25 minutes. Serve alone or drizzle each serving with beef gravy.

Tee Notes – If you'd like to make a gravy to drizzle onto your pie, here's an easy gravy recipe: use 1 tablespoon of butter, 2 tablespoons all-purpose flour, ¼ teaspoon garlic powder, 1/8 teaspoon salt, 1/8 teaspoons black pepper and 1 cup less sodium beef broth.

Melt butter in a small saucepan over medium heat; add flour and garlic, salt and pepper, stirring with a whisk. Slowly add broth, continue stirring until it is blended. Cook 2 minutes or until it thickens, stir constantly. Enjoy!

Notes

Notes

This is awesome sauce! I love this recipe so much. It's easy to make and very delicious. The chops are tender and the apple sauce is to live for. It is so good you'll want more, I promise you will!

CHOPS N' APPLE SAUCE

Serves 4

4 Golden Delicious apples, chopped

2 teaspoons lemon juice

¼ golden raisins

3 tablespoon light brown sugar

2 cups all natural cider, plus a splash for pan sauce

½ teaspoon ground cinnamon

¼ teaspoon freshly grated nutmeg

1 inch piece ginger root

4 tablespoons Tracye's Chicken Salad Dressing

1 tablespoon Virgin Olive Oil

4 (1- inch) thick center cut bone-in pork loin chops, 6 to 8 ounces each

Garlic and Pepper to taste

Combine first 8 ingredients in a medium pot placed over medium high heat and cook until a chunky sauce forms, 10 to 12 minutes, stirring occasionally. If sauce begin to splatter as it bubbles, reduce heat back a little, but it should be allowed to cook down and form into a sauce quickly. Once the apples are soft and sauce forms, remove it from the heat. If the sauce is too chunky, use a potato smasher to reduce to the consistency you'd like.

Heat a large nonstick skillet over medium high heat. Add Tracye's Chicken Salad Dressing to pan. Season chops on 1 side with pepper. Using a pair of tongs, add chops to hot skillet seasoned side down. Season the opposite side of the chops with garlic and pepper.

Brown the chops 2 minutes on each side, then reduce heat to medium and cook another 5 to 6 minutes, turning occasionally until juices run clear.

Remove chops from heat and let them rest a couple of minutes for juice to redistribute.

While the pan is hot put the 2 tablespoons of butter and a splash of apple juice or cider and 2 tablespoons of butter, stir to loosen brown bits from the bottom of the pan.

Pour pan sauce over chops.

Remove ginger from the applesauce and top the chops with the warm apple sauce.

Notes

I refer to this recipe as super easy breezy; Preparation and clean -up is a super breezy. Dinner will be served in about 20 minutes!

BAKED CHICKEN PARMESAN

4 Servings

4 Chicken tenders
1 jar of Tracye's Chicken Salad Dressing
1 ½ cup mozzarella cheese
¼ cup Parmesan cheese
Garlic powder
Ground black pepper

Preheat oven 350 degrees.

Place chicken tenders in a 13 x 9 baking dish. Season the chicken with garlic powder and ground black pepper.

Spread Tracye's Chicken Salad Dressing on top. Sprinkle the Parmesan cheese followed by the mozzarella cheese.

Bake uncovered for 20 minutes or until lightly brown.

This is great with brown rice, pasta or as a sandwich

Notes

_____

_____

_____

_____

_____

_____

_____

_____

_____

_____

IN BETWEEN

BOWL BURGER

BELLA BURGER

PORK-FECTION

CHICKEN SALAD MELT

ROAST BEEF

SEAFOOD ON A ROLL

When I decided to change my daily diet to low carb, I created the Bowl Burger. This fabulous burger is served without bread. It is so delicious that it will make you forget about the bun. It is so satisfying without filling over stuffed.

BOWL BURGER

Makes 4 Burgers

1 lb ground Sirloin beef
¼ Cup Tracye's Chicken Salad Dressing
¼ teaspoon ground black pepper
½ teaspoon garlic powder
½ teaspoon onion powder
4 slices of your favorite cheese (optional)

Combine Tracye's Chicken Salad Dressing, ground black pepper, garlic powder and onion powder in a bowl, mix well.

Add ground beef to the bowl and mix well; form 4 patties.

Grill, broil or cook on stove top.

Tee Notes – *Place everything you normally dress your burger with in a bowl. Place lots of lettuce in a bowl, followed by raw or grilled onions, tomatoes (sliced or cherry), ketchup, mustard and mayo. Place burger on the top of this, grab a fork and a knife, and dig in!*

Notes

Notes

This is a perfect meal for a meatless Monday. The Bella Burger is my grilled Portabella mushroom burger. It's delicious and easy to prepare.

BELLA BURGER

Makes 4 Burgers

4 Portobello mushroom caps
Tracye's Chicken salad Dressing
1 tablespoon minced garlic
Ground black pepper to taste
4 slices of Provolone cheese (or your favorite cheese)

Place the mushroom caps, smooth side up, in a shallow pan.

Brush 1Tablespoon of Tracye's Chicken Salad Dressing on each mushroom cap, ½ table spoon on each side. Let stand at room temperature for 10 minutes.

Preheat grill for medium-high heat.

Place mushrooms on the grill. Grill for 5 to 8 minutes on each side or until tender. Top with your cheese during the last 2 minutes of grilling.

Serve with lettuce, tomato slice, onion sliced thin and a light touch of Tracye's Chicken Salad Dressing

Tee Notes – Bella burger may also be broiled if you prefer not to grill.

Notes

Notes

If you follow these instructions, you will have "Pork-fection." The meat is so tender it seems to melt in your mouth. If you have any leftovers, divide it into portions and freeze it. Serve this with vegetables as a main course or as a sandwich on an onion roll, YUM!

PORK-FECTION

Serves 6

1 boneless Boston butt pork roast (about 3 ½ lbs)
1 medium onion
6 cloves fresh garlic
2 (14oz) cans reduced-sodium beef broth
½ cup cider vinegar
1 jar of Tracye's Chicken Salad Dressing
6 slices pepper jack cheese
6 Bakery French or regular Hamburger Rolls

Slice onion thickly, place in slow cooker* with garlic cloves. Stir in broth and cider vinegar. Add pork roast. Cover and cook on high 6-8 hours or until pork is fork tender.

You may cook in the oven at 400 degrees for 20 minutes, reduce temperature to 275 degrees for 3 hours.

Discard onions and garlic. Shred pork by using two forks or using gloved hands.

Pull the pork apart using your hands or 2 forks. Add Tracye's Chicken Salad Dressing to the pan of meat, mixing well.

Top your hot pulled pork with pepper jack cheese or a cheese of your choice

Place the meat on your favorite sandwich roll, and as one customer told me, it will be "good eating"

Tee Notes – *Place cooked pork roast in an aluminum shallow baking pan. Prepare a charcoal grill and smoke the roast for at least 45 minutes. DOUBLE YUM!*

Notes

Notes

Simply the best kept secret. Quick and easy, this is my version of the infamous grilled

CHICKEN SALAD MELT

Makes 1 sandwich

½ cup prepared chicken salad
2 slices Vermont cheddar cheese
Butter softened
Whole grain wheat bread

Generously butter 1 slice of bread and place it buttered side down into the skillet. Lay cheese slice on the slice of bread that is in the skillet; now put the chicken salad on top of the cheese, followed by another slice of cheese on top of the chicken salad. Butter the second slice of bread and place it on top of the sandwich, buttered side up.

Now grill at medium heat until lightly brown and flip over; continue grilling until cheese is melted.

Tee Notes – Make sure you grill on low heat otherwise the bread will be oh so pretty golden brown and the cheese and chicken salad will give you the cold shoulder because it was not able to heat.

Notes

Notes

Super easy roast beef sandwich that is really tasty. The caramelized onions really set this apart from other roast beef sandwiches.

ROAST BEEF

Makes 4 sandwiches

1 pound thinly sliced roast beef
6 tablespoons thinly sliced red onion
2 tablespoons Tracye's Chicken Salad Dressing
4 yeast rolls

Heat 2 tablespoons of Tracye's Chicken Salad Dressing in a skillet over medium heat, add onions and caramelize*.

Slice yeast rolls and put roast beef slices on, one slice at a time (3 to 4 slices per sandwich). Top with caramelized onion and 1 teaspoon of Tracye's Chicken Salad Dressing.

Tee Notes – Caramelize onions by heating them slowly. Onions are naturally sweet. When you slowly cook onions over an extended period of time, the natural sugars in the onion caramelize, turning brown. Do not try and rush by raising the heat. Be patient, it will only take about 5 min or so. Trust me it's worth the wait. You can also use caramelized onions atop of steak, onion soup, pizzas and more.

Notes

_____

_____

_____

_____

_____

_____

_____

_____

_____

_____

Notes

This seafood roll is heavenly. It is so simple yet so good. I tell you the best things in life are simple.

SEAFOOD ON A ROLL

4 servings

Yeast slider rolls
1 lobster tail
1 pound medium shrimp peeled and deveined
Celery chopped
4 tablespoons Tracye's Chicken Salad Dressing

Pre-heat oven on Broil

Slit tops of rolls but not all the way through, and butter roll

Remove meat from lobster and cut into small chunks,

Put Tracye's Chicken Salad Dressing in a skillet over medium high heat

Add celery and cook for 2 minutes, then add seafood. Cook seafood until done, frequently tossing it to coat it with the dressing, (the dressing will turn into oil and the herbs in the dressing will adhere to the seafood).

Place the butter rolls in the oven, remove after the butter has melted and the rolls are lightly toasted. Fill each roll with the seafood mixture and enjoy!

Tee notes – you may also use precooked frozen seafood medleys instead of fresh/raw seafood. Just be sure not to heat it to long otherwise it will be rubbery.

Notes

Notes

ON THE SIDE

NOT SO CREAMY SPINACH

JUST GREEN BEANS

ROASTED CAULIFLOWER

OVEN ROASTED POTATOES

BAKED TWICE
SPAGHETTI SQUASH

PAN-FRIED ASPARAGUS

SMASHED POTATOES

Preparing vegetables with my chicken salad dressing is amazing. Each vegetable has its own unique flavor when the dressing is applied thus making vegetable preparation so quick and easy that even a child could do it!

This is the second recipe developed with my dressing. It was a lazy afternoon and yours truly wanted some creamed spinach. I didn't feel like pulling out the cream, butter, nutmeg, and all the other ingredients to make creamed spinach. I picked up the jar of dressing and wondered what it would taste like with spinach," I made the recipe below and loved the taste as well as the short time it took to prepare...check it out below!

NOT SO CREAMY SPINACH

Serves 4

8 cups fresh spinach
4 Tablespoons Tracye's Chicken Salad Dressing
4 teaspoons minced garlic
Parmesan Cheese to taste

In a large sauce pan, place spinach, dressing and garlic. Cook over medium high heat.

Stir to coat the spinach with the dressing; continue to stir until the spinach has wilted.

Add Parmesan cheese, toss to incorporate it with the spinach and serve! You may sprinkle additional parmesan cheese atop spinach for garnish.

Notes

Notes

Green beans are a snap when you fix them with my dressing - no butter or salt needed!

JUST GREEN BEANS

Serves 6

1 ½ pounds green beans
½ red bell pepper, chopped
4 tablespoons Tracye's Chicken Salad Dressing
½ teaspoon ground black pepper

Preheat the oven to 425 F.

Trim the ends of the green beans and add to a large bowl

Toss with Tracye's Chicken Salad Dressing, coating the green beans. Sprinkle pepper. Put green beans in a baking dish, sprinkle red bell pepper on top and cover with foil.

Bake covered for 30 minutes or tender with a crunch.

Tee Notes – *for a little extra flavor and nutritional value, add diced tomatoes for garnish.*

The green beans may also be prepared on the stove top. Cook green beans as you normally would, then toss them in a heated pan with my dressing and serve.

Notes

Notes

Even though this recipe was developed as a side dish, it can stand alone as a healthy snack. The marriage between my dressing and the grated Parmesan cheese is a match made in heaven!

ROASTED CAULIFLOWER

Serves 4

2 tablespoons minced garlic
1 large head cauliflower separated into florets
½ cup Tracye's Chicken Salad Dressing
1/3 cup grated Parmesan cheese
Pepper to taste
1 tablespoon chopped fresh parsley

Preheat the oven to 450 degrees. Grease a large casserole dish

Place Tracye's Chicken Salad Dressing and garlic in a large re-sealable bag; add cauliflower, and shake to mix. Pour into the prepared casserole dish. Season with salt and pepper to taste.

Bake for 25 minutes, stirring halfway through. Top with Parmesan cheese and parsley, and broil for 3-5 minutes, until golden brown.

Tee Notes – *be sure to keep close watch during the broiling stage to make sure they don't burn.*

Notes

This recipe is wonderful. Forget about the butter and sour cream. Use my dressing on your potato and the potato as we've known it can be history. The potato is healthy once again!

OVEN ROASTED POTATOES

4 Servings

1 1/2 pounds baby Yukon Gold potatoes
1 teaspoons freshly ground pepper
4 Tablespoons of Tracye's Chicken Salad Dressing

Preheat oven to 425 degrees F.

Slice the bottom off each potato and cut crosswise at 1/8-inch intervals, cutting 1/4 inch of the bottom.

Arrange the potatoes on a sheet pan cut side up.

Bake the potatoes for 20 minuites, until they are tender. Remove from the oven and spread a thin layer of Tracye's Chicken Salad Dressing over each potato. Return potatoes to the oven and bake for an additional 10 minutes until they are golden and crisp on top.

Tee Notes – *Place the potato on a large spoon so the edges of the spoon prevent you from slicing completely through the potato.*

Notes

Notes

Eat all the spaghetti you want, it's okay because it's really a vegetable. Unlike pasta, it's not a starch, and is naturally gluten free. When I first tried it I fell in love with it. It has a very subtle sweet taste. Don't be afraid, go ahead and try this one.

BAKED TWICE SPAGHETTI SQUASH

Serves 4

1 large spaghetti squash
2 cloves garlic
¼ teaspoon pepper
½ cup Parmesan cheese
½ jar Tracye's Chicken Salad Dressing

Preheat oven 350. Wash the skin of the squash. Using a sharp knife, slice the squash in half, lengthwise from stem to tail. Scoop out seeds and discard. Pour a little water in the pan, enough to cover the bottom. Lay the squash halves on the baking sheet, flesh side down. Bake for 30-45 minutes.

While the squash bakes, combine garlic, pepper, parmesan cheese and ½ cup Tracye's Chicken Salad Dressing in a mixing bowl, set aside.

Check squash after 30 minutes to gauge cooking. Squash is done when the skin is tender and you can pierce it with a fork. Using a fork, gently pull the squash flesh from the peel. ~Save the peel, carefully rake your fork in the same direction as the strands to make the longest "noodles." Place them in a bowl. Combine dressing mixture with the spaghetti squash. Return the squash to the skins. Lightly sprinkle additional parmesan cheese on top. Return to the oven and bake for 10 minutes or until it's golden brown and serve.

Tee Notes – *Instead of cutting the squash in half, you can also roast it whole. Roast until a fork can easily pierce through the outer peel and all the way to the interior of the squash, about an hour. Slice in half and carefully remove the seeds and stringy flesh, then scrape the flesh as directed above.*

Notes

I tried asparagus for the first time about 15 years ago on Chicken Madeira, OMG! I didn't know what I was missing. I've been hooked ever since. An asparagus recipe was a must. This is a very simple recipe that I'm confident asparagus and not so asparagus lovers will enjoy.

PAN-FRIED ASPARAGUS

4 Servings

1 bunch fresh asparagus
3 cloves garlic
3 tablespoons Tracye's Chicken Salad Dressing

Heat Tracye's Chicken Salad Dressing in a large skillet over medium high heat

Add the garlic and asparagus spears; cover and cook for 10 minutes, or until asparagus is tender, tossing occasionally while cooking.

Remove asparagus and serve!

Tee Notes – If you like your asparagus well done, reduce the heat and cook an additional 10 minutes.

Notes

Notes

Smashed is what we call these mashed potatoes. This is a favorite among my clients. A week doesn't go by without this being on the menu. If you love good old fashioned mashed potatoes this is the perfect recipe. Easy and Tee-licious!

SMASHED POTATOES

Serves 4

2 pounds baking potatoes, peeled and quartered
½ cup Tracyes Chicken Salad Dressing
1 teaspoon garlic powder
Fresh parsley, garnish

Bring a pot of water to a boil

Add potatoes and cook until tender, about 15 minutes, drain.

Add chicken salad dressing and garlic to the hot potatoes

Mash potatoes using a potato masher until smooth.

Salt and pepper to taste (optional)

Tee Notes – Be sure to taste the potatoes before adding salt, it may not need it, it depends on your taste buds.

Notes

Notes

ABOUT THE AUTHOR

Tracye Carter was born to cook. During her childhood years in Wisconsin, she'd always accompany her mother grocery shopping on Saturday mornings. It is there that Tracye learned the art of choosing the best produce, meats, and comparison shopping for a balanced meal. With the guidance of her mother, Tracye learned to cook delicious meals and baked goods from scratch.

In 1988, Tracye relocated to Georgia, with starting a business in her view. After careful consideration, she wanted to do something that she was passionate about. It didn't take long for her to realize her love for the domestic side of life. In 1992, she started her own domestic services company, Cleanique Cleaning, followed by Simply Elegance Catering in 1994. Tracye's domestic businesses were devoted to being economical and detailed oriented. She was devoted to providing healthy yet delicious home-cooked foods and desserts for a variety of facilities and events.

In 2009, Tracye became a preferred caterer for Georgia State University as well as countless active adult living facilities and community organizations. This has helped Tracye become a top caterer in the Atlanta area.

When Tracye received a catering request for chicken salad, she decided to make a homemade recipe featuring a combination of tasty yet healthy ingredients. Her chicken salad was a hit, and word spread. People began asking her to share her recipe. Rather than give up her time-honored recipe, Tracye decided to create a simple solution that would allow clients to duplicate her chicken salad at home. She created a chicken salad dressing that could simply be added to cooked chicken to make an amazing chicken salad.

She has now developed recipes that are healthy, quick, and easy, saving the user precious time and energy.

In addition to being an entrepreneur, Tracye is also an executive pastor at New Life Christian Fellowship in Racine, Wisconsin, a mentor to young girls and cooking instructor.

CPSIA information can be obtained
at www.ICGtesting.com
Printed in the USA
LVOW05s2339040216

473763LV00021B/150/P